The Korean Spirit

The Korean Spirit
Poems

H. C. Kim

Koreani

Highland Park   Seoul   Bangalore   Cebu City

The Korean Spirit: Poems

All Rights Reserved © 2007 by H. C. Kim

No part of this book may be reproduced or transmitted in any form or by any means, graphic, electronic, or mechanical, including photocopying, recording, taping, or by any information storage retrieval system, without the permission in writing from the publisher.

For information address:

Koreani Press
12325 Imperial Highway
Suite 156
Norwalk, California 90650
United States of America
info@KoreaniPress.com

http://www.KoreaniPress.com

ISBN: 1-59689-071-1

Library of Congress Cataloging-in-Publication Data

Kim, H. C. (Heerak Christian)
 The Korean spirit : poems / H.C. Kim.
    p. cm.
 ISBN 1-59689-071-1 (pbk. : alk. paper)
 1. Koreans--Poetry. I. Title.
 PS3611.I4544K67 2007
 811'.6--dc22
                                    2007021060

Dedicated to the Memory of

Ae-Ju Ham
My maternal grandmother

Who grew up without a father who was killed by the
Japanese Army when she was 1 year old
For fighting for Korean Independence

Who herself was arrested by the Japanese Army
In her teenage years because she demonstrated
On behalf of Korean Independence

"None of us know all the potentialities
that slumber in the spirit of the population,
or all the ways in which that population can surprise us
when there is the right interplay of events."

Vaclav Havel
Writer, Thinker, Revolutionary
The first President of the Czech Republic (1993-2003)

Contents

"A Group Prayer" /1/
"And the Glory" /3/
"And the Power" /5/
"Apologies" /7/
"Busted" /9/
"But Deliver Us" /10/
"Celebration" /12/
"Chicago Businessman" /14/
"Comfort Women" /15/
"Crowded City" /17/
"Daepodong 2" /19/
"Date 'em and Leave 'em" /21/
"Defamation" /24/
"Disillusioned" /26/
"Early Morning Prayer" /28/
"Evacuation" /30/
"For Thine" /32/
"Forever, Amen" /34/
"Forgive Us Our Debts" /35/
"From Evil" /38/
"From the North" /40/
"German Korean" /42/
"German Korean Youth" /43/
"Give Us This Day" /45/
"God Will Protect" /47/
"Grandma" /49/

Contents

"Han River" /51/
"Have No English" /53/
"Her Hair" /54/
"Her Skin" /55/
"Holy Be Your Name" /57/
"Inopportune Time" /59/
"Inside the Dry Cleaner's" /61/
"Into Temptation" /63/
"Is the Kingdom" /67/
"It Wasn't the Car" /69/
"Japanese Informers" /71/
"Japanese Police" /73/
"Japanese Testimony" /74/
"Koreatown" /75/
"Korean Outreach" /76/
"Korean Restaurant Owner" /78/
"Korean Ways" /80/
"Koreans Hear" /82/
"Koreaspeak" /84/
"LA Riots" /85/
"Laughing at Heaven" /87/
"Lead Us Not" /89/
"UCLA Korean Student" /91/
"Little Girl" /92/
"Loyalty" /94/
"Martyr" /96/
"Meaning" /98/
"Meaningless" /100/
"No Korea" /102/
"North Korea Missionary" /104/
"Not Naïve" /106/
"On Earth As In Heaven" /108/

Contents

"One Dead" /111/
"One Wish" /113/
"Our Daily Bread" /115/
"Our Father in Heaven" /117/
"Private War" /118/
"Remember" /120/
"Segregated Cafeteria" /121/
"Seoul" /123/
"Street Battle" /125/
"The Bullet Wound" /127/
"The Date" /129/
"The Good Son" /131/
"The Immigrant" /133/
"The Invasion" /134/
"The Korean War" /136/
"The Mirror" /138/
"The Model Immigrant" /139/
"The Stranger" /141/
"The Unrighteous" /143/
"The Voice of the Silent" /145/
"Three Korean Women" /148/
"Thy Kingdom Come" /149/
"Thy Will Be Done" /151/
"To Testify" /153/
"Trespass" /155/
"Truth" /156/
"Unexpected Attack" /158/
"Victory" /160/
"What's In It For Me?" /162/
"Why Hate?" /164/
"Widowed" /165/
"Wonder" /167/

Contents

"Yacht" /169/

Preface

Koreans around the world are going through profound changes. Some of this is due to the dynamics of global politics and the rapprochement of South Korea and North Korea. Some of this is due to the changing "open" global market place and the global "village." Yet, some is due to the mystery of the human experience that sometimes exhibits itself in communal participation and collective (sub-)consciousness. This collection of poems captures a bit of this confused Korean experience.

H. C. Kim
57th Anniversary of the Korean War
Elizabeth, New Jersey
United States of America

The Korean Spirit

"A Group Prayer"

They prayed together
A group prayer
Those who have never been to Korea
Born in the US of A
For the sake of Korean unification

They had a Korean soul
Born of a Korean father and a Korean mother
They knew of distant relatives
Whom they have never met
Still suffering in North Korea as Christians

They prayed for God's work
To unify the North and the South
For the governments have failed
Japan threatens Korea with attack
America backing Japan up

Like 100 years ago
When Japan wanted to conquer Korea
Colonized it
America made a backroom deal with Japan
To put Korea under Japanese rule

Korans trusted America
After all
A Christian country
Will not sell us out
Would they?

But they did
The US government sold Korea out
And after 35 years of slavery under Japan

America helped chop Korea into two
North and South

There is no one to turn to
South Korean government is corrupt
US government cannot be trusted
Japan wants to conquer Korea again
Only God is our help

They prayed a group prayer
Trusting that God can unite
North Korea and South Korea
Before Japan and USA team up
To destroy Korea and kill Koreans in the North

"And the Glory"

And the glory is mine!
Yelled the power hungry dictator
Who has abused power
To gain a stronghold
In Korean politics

He lavished the rich with influence
Winning their allegiance to himself
He showed judges and politicians
With money that corrupts
To win their support

He paraded before the poor
With star-studded entourage
Making himself out to be a celebrity
He bribed the police with evil
And judges with dubious favors

The evil dictator gained ascendancy
And amassed more and more power
As no one was vigilant enough to understand
Honorable enough to stand up
Giving enough to resist

And the glory became his
So it seemed
As he paraded before the poor
Temporarily winning their accolade
Although many invisibly harbored disgust

Slowly protest emerged
Among the decent folk
Who just had enough

And the bullet flew
And took him off Korean politics

"And the Power"

And the power
Where is the power?
Do you know?
Have you seen it?
Abused?

Power corrupts
And absolute power
Corrupts absolutely
On earth
A fallible realm

Have you seen a king corrupted?
By money thrown in his direction
Fame and glory
All he could see
Blinding his good will

Like Saul
In the Book of Samuel
King appointed by God
Corrupted through power
Refusing to do good

Where is the power in our country?
Should President Park
Be allowed to remain in power forever
Abusing the rights of Korean citizens
Oppressing the poor?

Will a deliverer come
To save the Korean people
From the grips of a makeshift dictator

H. C. Kim

Who refuses to care
About the cry of the downtrodden?

"Apologies"

Apologies uttered as a formality
Is that only what Asians will hear
Sorries without content or meaning
They won't change history

Nor will they improve the Asian condition
In a university system
Devoid of viable Asian faculty presence
Nor high ranking Asian administrators

40% of the university students are Asian
So Asians should be happy
At the lack of Asian professors
Dearth of Asian administrators

Be satisfied with tuition-paying Asian students
Who color the campus Asian
Yes, they have no real vote on university direction
Nor can they put more Asians in power

But they are visible
And boy, are they visible!
You can see those speak
Who want to keep Asian leadership at a minimum

Asian students oblivious to the problem
Walk, talk, eat, and go to class
Thinking there's no problem
But they will see

When they are in the real world
That the fight they did not start
On a micro-community of their university

Will cost them their job and future potential

"Busted"

Busted
Is the American dream
He carried in his heart
As his wife carried his son
In her womb

Flying
Through the blue skies
East to west
Old to new
Or was it?

Now
Remembering
The Korean immigrant
Smiles
A bittersweet pain

Grown
Is the son
Who was the hope
For which
He uprooted

Discarded
Is his son
By a white world
Condemning his Korean face
Along with his Ivy League qualifications

"But Deliver Us"

We bowed down to the flag
But deliver us
Korean Christian prayed
As they faced their imminent death

It was not like we opposed Christ directly
They try to reason with God
In group prayer
They knew sure death was coming

North Koreans are just a few miles away!
They heard someone shout outside
They are killing everyone in sight
It's like the plague of Egypt

We bowed down to the flag
But it was under duress
Or out of respect
It was not like we were more loyal to the flag

The sound of bombs came closer
And the planes and war machines
Made their terrible noises
The tragedy advanced day after day

We bowed to the flag
But did not worship it like an idol
We know our nation is not Christian
But we think it was okay

Korean Christians gathered around
As North Koreans approached
Repenting of bowing down

The Korean Spirit: Poems

To the South Korean flag

"Celebration"

Today is a day of celebration
For I saw an enemy killed today
With my own eyes
A brave young man
Risking his life and freedom

Today is a day of celebration
Because he joined the army
To kill the enemy
Out of his own free will
Knowing of the dangers

Today is a day of celebration
Because one of them is dead
Many besides myself have seen it
And still others hear about it
What a joyful day!

We are a people suffering
Under the yolk of oppression
They invaded our land
Trampled upon our ways
And show no respect to our values

We wanted peace
But they wanted war
We wanted to share kindness
But they wanted to poison our food
They worked to intimidate us

And now their invasion has met its match
Private citizens like him
Others joining as well

Willing to take a weapon
To protest their rude invasion

South Koreans are a brave people
And we will celebrate
The death of an enemy
Who represents all that is evil
And offensive to our ways

H. C. Kim

"Chicago Businessman"

The Chicago businessman stood
There in front of over a thousand faces
Korean-American teens
And thought to himself
I was like them once

The Korean-American businessman asked himself
What can I say
To give them courage
To defend the Korean-American community
And shine like the Turtleship of Korean history?

He had planned to talk
Giving a politically correct speech
Without much content
But that would make him look good
His investors look good

Then, he thought to himself
These faces represent Korea's future
They are the future leaders
Of me, you, and all Korean-Americans
I can't betray my community

I will say something meaningful
Which will make them think
And when they grow up
They will point to this moment
As one that changed their life

"Comfort Women"

They called them
Comfort Women
Prostitutes in fact
Name changed for their benefit

Not the benefit of the women
But of the soldiers
Who fought in the battlefield
On behalf of the imperialist power

With a constructive title
East Asia Co-Prosperity Sphere
Everyone asked
Where's the "Co"?

Japan seized power
In the name of pan-Asian movement
And colonized Korea
Attacked the Chinese

Asian women
From China and Korea
Sent as prostitutes
For the East Asia Co-Prosperity Sphere

A euphemism
For Japan's right
To absolute domination
In Asia and beyond

Asian women
Arrested for no reason
Except that they were beautiful

Their family poverty exploited

Asian women
Sent to work as sex slaves
For Japanese soldiers
To render their service every day

Asian women
In the tens of thousands
Even hundreds
Who became official prostitutes

Comfort women
Greatest number from Korea
They brought comfort
Alright

Not to themselves
Nor their families
Nor to their nation
Only to those who oppressed them

"Crowded City"

Have you been to Seoul
The crowded city
And think to yourself
What if?

What if the North invaded?
How many Koreans would die
In one hour
Maybe a million or two?

If you haven't been to Seoul
You can't understand
But a barrage of missiles
150 rockets fired?

They would kill hundreds of thousands
One tall apartment building destroyed
Would kill thousands or more
And 150?

In one hour
Missiles plus panic
Plus all that fire
Going from building to building

Stampede
Cars running into each other
Mayhem
Riots and looting everywhere

In an hour or two
Millions may die
Seoul is a concentrated area

Where are the people going to go?

North Korea invades
The crowded city
More crowded than New York
Even more than Hong Kong

In a few hours
Millions dead
And the capital destroyed
Blood everywhere

North Korea would conquer the South
In a few days
If they launched a surprise attack
Like the Korean War

Where will all the Seoulites go?
To death and then some
In a few hours
Half the city would be dead

"Daepodong 2"

Daepodong 2
In preparation
Being loaded to be fired
The world condemns
The Korean boy exults

Why do you exult, little boy?
Because that's made in Korea
It's the first missile designed by Koreans
That can travel through the Pacific
Bridge two nations in its flight

Don't you know that it can kill?
Yeah, but it can only kill lives
It can't kill the soul or the spirit
My Korean spirit is assaulted in school
By white classmates who look down on Koreans

You should not hate them
No, I don't
It is they who hate me
It is they who rejected me
It is they who disenfranchise me

So you are going to side with North Korea?
It's not about taking sides
I am Korean
I take pleasure at Korean advancement
It's a technological advancement

It's an evil empire!
What is evil?
The boy who is arrested for stealing bread

Does his mother think he is evil?
I am a Korean, you see

North Korea should focus on food!
How could it
When there are all these sanctions?
They have no choice
But to defend itself

We don't'see it that way
I know you don't
You are not Korean
You do not have a Korean soul
You can't understand

"Date 'em and Leave 'em"

She complained to her friend
Of her own kind
About an experience
She recently had

Why do they
Date 'em and leve 'em?
Her friend nodded
Understanding what she meant

Don't you see
We are yellow people
Of different skin
And identity

Yeah, but what does that matter?
Love conquers all
Don't it?
It shouldn't matter to him

What did he tell ya?
That you are too different?
That would have been semi-honest
Or did he give you one of his lies?

What do you mean?
He is a nice guy
He wouldn't lie to me
Would he?

All guys lie
For different reasons
But they have lies

Reserved for Korean girls like you and me

Korean girls like you and me?
What do you mean?
Korean-American women
Seeking meaningful relationships?

Yeah, Korean-Americans dating white men
They like to date us
Because we are different
They want to try something new

You can't dismiss all white men
Can you?
How could you?
They are not all the same

To me
They are all the same
Because I hear the same story
After story from Korean women like you

And you are saying
I am not alone?
That other Korean-American women
Tread the path I have suffered?

You betcha!
They have also experienced
Love 'em and leave 'em
Their exotic experience with a Korean

You mean to tell me
That they never meant anything serious?
Long-term relationship and marriage?
That they just used me?

Don't be naïve girl
You have been burned
But let that be a lesson to you
They will always find an excuse to dump you

Here, I was
Trying to escape
My Korean-American identity
I guess I can't escape my color

"Defamation"

What manner of defamation is this?
When they think they have the right
To reign on our soil
And disrespect our history
Our origins when we are the majority

This is our land
Which we have built up for centuries
Our blood runs through this soil
Our faith has kept our people alive
What right do they have to impose themselves on us?

This land is our land
This land is not your land
You feel you have the right to occupy our land
To govern us from positions of power
And subjugate our people

You who are less than 2 per cent of the population
Think you have the right to control the 98%?
You deserve to die
And we'll kill you
For our nation belongs to us

What manner of defamation is this?
To forbid us to speak our language
To express our collective thoughts as one people
With common shared history
Who have built this land for centuries?

Just because you are now elites in our land
You have high education
And control the government

Manipulating our people
Paying some off and threatening others

You have no right to our land
We will kill you
With guns, knives, or physical attacks
We will use our own hands to end your life
For you have oppressed ours

We are one people
Who are the majority
And this land is ours
Your elite population does not have the right
To govern us and force your ideology on us

Koreans shouted in their hearts
To reclaim their land
Downtrodden for 35 years
Under the rule of the Japanese
Who called themselves elite

"Disillusioned"

The Korean preacher had become disillusioned
After years of sacrifice
Taking all kinds of dirt from everybody
And not seeing a progress
In the Korean-American community

With a heavy heart
He went to the Korean Christian conference
Because he wanted to watch over his kids
Teenagers at a susceptible age
He did not trust the youth pastor

Day after day
He watched his children like a hawk
They were all he had left
What would happen
If they fell into the hands of Satan?

He could not bear it
He would consider his ministry a complete failure
If his children went away from Christ
He was disillusioned with the Korean community
But he had hope in Christ still

Night after night
He attended the nightly revival meeting
Sermons preached by a young Korean-American pastor
He saw himself in his sermons
He had that kind of zeal once

The day came
When the young preacher called
For a missionary to North Korea

None stood up
Only one to go to the bathroom

Strangely enough
He felt tears welling up in his eyes
And felt the hot tears down his cheeks
Without knowing
He stood up to everyone's surprise

Dad!
He heard his son cry in desperation
What are we going to do?
He heard his daughter cried
They had no shame for they were scared

The disillusioned pastor walked up
And faced his children and the youth
Their eyes focused on him
And the young preacher was in shock
But happy that someone responded

I will go
For my people
To bring the Gospel
To preach the good news
To hungry souls

To die for Christ
If need be for the heavenly crown
Of a faithful servant
Who has risked his life for the LORD
I commit myself

"Early Morning Prayer"

Early in the morning
They gathered for prayer
An age old Korean tradition
Some say started in Korean churches

Right now
Our parents are gathered for prayer
In the wee hours in the morning
Korean churches gather for prayer

In the United States
In South Korea
In Great Britain
In Russia, too

The teens gathered for prayers
Not often done back home
But it's a Korean Christian camp
And they are here fore spiritual rejuvenation

One by one
They trickled in
Before the sun came up
To a room for prayer and praise

Eyes barely open
Some with their shirts backwards
From college age
To those barely out of elementary school

They are here for a Christian youth celebration
Of the cross and all Christ have done for Korea
To get nearer to Christ personally

And grow in the Christian faith

Soon, the whole room was filled
With those who wanted to worship Jesus Christ
And submit to the rule of Christ the King
In their life and as a community

"Evacuation"

The civilians waited their evacuation
This is not our war
We were here peacefully
Enjoying a nice summer day

People here are nice
And so friendly
Offering us their tea
And friendship everywhere we go

They do not deserve this invasion
We are on their side
The victims of military aggression
Why should these civilians fear

They didn't start a war
Their government did not start the war
Even the most extremists among them
Did not start a military invasion

But the other side
Had other plans
For the people they considered
The Other

They did not care
Whether they killed civilians
In fact, they targeted
Civilian sites

Many civilians died
Our friends
People who know friendship

And generosity

And here we are
Americans
Awaiting evacuation
Because the other side invaded

"For Thine"

For Thine is the Kingdom
The young boy prayed
His Lord's Prayer
And stopped to look up

He wondered what this meant
It was the first time he had stopped to think
Words were uttered robotically before
Now it rang something inside

For Thine is the Kingdom
This ain't true!
The boy yelled
And surprised his father next to him

Be quiet little boy!
His father said
And looked around the room to see
Eyes gazed upon him

But, dad, this isn't true!
The kingdom belongs to the Japanese
The kingdom of Korea belongs to Japan
They killed the Korean king!

Tears ran down the father's cheeks
He meant to tell his boy
The kingdom is not referring to Korea
But the innocent truth of the boy awakened him

It was true
The kingdom of Korea did not belong to God
It belonged to the Japanese

And the latent anger was stirred in his heart

It was that day
The father decided
To protest the Japanese rule
The kingdom of Korea should belong to God

H. C. Kim

"Forever, Amen"

I want to live forever, Amen!
I heard the policeman yell
He was slightly drunk
Actually very drunk

He had been carousing
And letting off steam
As he says
And he bragged about his power

And the gun he carried at his side
He thought no one could touch him
Not even God
I want to live forever, Amen!

The policeman walked
Jumped and hopped
Along the street
Thinking that he was not a human being

Then he came to the ally way
And bang he heard a sound
Not of a joyful firecracker
But a bullet that took his Japanese soul

"Forgive Us Our Debts"

We have incurred a large debt
As a country
Because we strive to fight the war
In the Name of Christ Jesus
To defend the Body of Christ

We have seen what the Japanese did
In assailing the church
Legislating against the Christian faith
In the name of toleration of religion
They forced their national symbol into our sanctuary

Like the government owned the worshipping place
Of the LORD Jesus Christ
Whose Name be forever praised
They thought it treacherous
That the church opposed the national symbol in worship

How many Koreans died
A Christian martyr's death
Standing against the government
Trying to impose their secular power
Inside the worship place

The government dared to think
They can carry out their security exercises
Inside the church of Jesus Christ
Which is not under their jurisdiction
A place that honors Christ

The government has insulted Christ
By sending their agents into the church
To get the pastors to comply with government issues

What do they think the church is?
Do they think they own Christ our LORD?

Many Christians refused to cooperate
Because they were loyal to Christ
Not to the government
Or to their security agencies
Who dared to insult Christ by carrying on their activities

North Korea will do the same
As they occupy South Korea
This war is a fight to the finish
To impose their government policy
Upon the Church of Jesus Christ

We learned our lesson
Under the Japanese occupation
We will not sit idly by
As the Church of Jesus Christ
Is conquered and abused by the government

In the name of national security
The Japanese government did what they pleased
Imposed themselves upon our worship program
Placed their agents in the church
And disrupted worship honoring Christ the LORD

We will incur national debt
Personal debt
Family debt
To wage war in the Name of Jesus Christ
So the government cannot come in and insult Christ

Forgive us our debt
Pay our debt on our behalf
Because this debt was incurred

On behalf of Christ and the Kingdom of Christ
Vengeance is Mine saith the LORD

H. C. Kim

"From Evil"

From evil we were delivered
Korean Christians yelled
At American missionaries
Fundamentalist Christians who returned

Who taught them to mistrust the government
Secular government which does not respect Christ
The Kingdom of Christ
Or its rule on this earth

The American missionaries told them
Not to vote or participate in politics
The government was evil
It corrupted true Christians who entered it

From evil we were delivered
Korean Christian emphasized
American Christian missionaries
Asked them what they meant

The devout evangelical Christian president
Syngman Rhee of South Korea
Became corrupt in politics
And denied Christian law its rightful place

After becoming Christian
South Korea became more secular
Christian laws pushed aside
In the name of national security

You are right
Fundamentalist Christians of America
For saying that politics corrupts

It corrupted a so-called evangelical who wanted to please

President Syngman Rhee cared about power
Not about his submission to Christ the King of kings
He concerned himself not with the rule of Christ in the land
And went on a tolerance trip

From evil of this so-called evangelical Christian president
Who neither upheld Christ's honor or supported His rule
We are free!
We are delivered from evil of his anti-Christian rule

H. C. Kim

"From the North"

From the North
A swarm of locusts
Entered the land
Covering it completely dark

One could not see the skies
But the flying objects
Quickly approaching
And there was devastation in the land

Koreans never thought this would happen
They assumed that they would be safe
That God would protect them
But the North Korean army invaded

With a surprise
And no warning
They came down south
Like the plague of Egypt

On a Sunday
Before morning worship services began
As if God wanted to send a message
I don't want your corrupt worship

Koreans have quickly forgotten
That God wants obedience rather than sacrifice
Upholding the glory of Christ rather than a worship service
Loyalty only to the Kingdom of Christ

A few years after the celebration
Ending of the Japanese Occupation
Cozy Korea was hit against

But this time with millions of dead South Koreans

From the North
Came destruction
As the swarm of locusts passed by
Dead bodies marked their path

"German Korean"

You thought there were no German Koreans
Living in the land of plenty
Millions of Koreans
Albeit outside Korea

No, you are wrong
There are Koreans
Spread out across the Vaterland
Many born there

Fluent in German
Conversant in Korean
Attending Korean churches
Trying to build a Korean community there

Struggling with issues of identity
Not unlike those you face in America
Being Korean yet belonging outside
Neither being part of the Motherland

There are German Koreans
Lots of them
And the numbers are increasing
They are shining like stars in Germany

"German Korean Youth"

German Korean Youth sat there
Jiving in German
Acting like Germans in every way
But they looked Korean
Even more Korean
Than the FOB's I saw in San Francisco
Going to a language school
To get into Berkeley
Like their mom and dad dream
They are Korean in appearance
But German in every other way
Even though they speak Korean
Many being quite fluent
Yet they do not see
Their mixed identity
For there is confusion
Generation gap from first to second
Transition in Korea doesn't help
They are like lost sheep
Jiving in German
Trying to feel Korean
Confused about their identity
Korean church helps
To find their way
For the Korean church
Gives them their communal identity
Which they don't find
In their journeys
Far and wide
East and west
They are like lost sheep
Floating on the high sea
Wind blows this way and that

And they are pushed from one side to the next
There doesn't seem to be hope
But they will land
In the island of hope
For they have faith
In the God of Koreans
Whom they worship
For whom blood of Korean martyrs was shed
From the beginning of Korean church history
Men and women of faith
Who recreated Korean identity
Along Christian lines

"Give Us This Day"

Give us this day
The courage to stand up
Stand up for the Name of Christ
And His Body, the Church

South Korean Christian soldiers uttered
As they faced battle
And many
A certain death

We fight a power
Greater than us
We are outnumbered
We are outgunned

The Communists
Have more sophisticated weapons
Their advanced tanks have entered
Our southern region

They fight to gain land
To create a greater buffer zone
We want to live
To worship you in Your church

Jesus Christ our LORD
Who is King of kings
And the LORD of lords
Whosoever believes in him shall not perish

But have eternal life
Give us today
Our courage

Which we need to face death

The courage to kill
The enemy of Christ
Who seeks to destroy the Christian church
And persecute Christians

We fight
Not for our country
But for the Kingdom of Christ
The Body of Christ in South Korea

Communists already have their tanks
Those who hate Jesus Christ
Refuse to acknowledge that He is God
They have entered our southern region

May these enemies of Christ die
And fall by our guns
Although they are more powerful than we
Give us this day the courage to kill

"God Will Protect"

God will protect!
The little boy
Heard the preacher preach from the pulpit

And he wondered to himself
As young as he was
What does that mean?

Will God protect Korea
Like He protected Koreans
In the Japanese Occupation?

Will God protect Korea
Like He protected Koreans
In the Korean War?

Will God protect Korea
Like He protected Los Angeles Koreans
In the L.A. Riots?

Will God protect Korea
Like He protected Chicago's Korean merchants
After the Cubs victories?

Will God protect Korea
Like He protected the father of those two
Who was shot dead in a carjacking?

What if?
Maybe God doesn't want to protect Korea
Perhaps God wants to punish Korea

Who can fathom the mind of God?

The little boy thought
Does the preacher know what he is talking about?

God doesn't owe Koreans anything?
The Japanese Occupation showed that
And the Korean War showed God's not scared

We can't bully God into protecting us
We can't command God into protecting us
We can't bribe God into protecting us

What's in it for God?
The boy asked himself
Does the preacher even know?

"Grandma"

The Korean girl remembered
As she sat in a room full of Korean people
The story of her grandma
How she marched in the March 1st Movement
During the Japanese Occupation

She used to talk with her
All the time
When she was alive
She spoke in Korean
But could not read or write Korean

The Japanese forced us to learn Japanese
They required us to speak only Japanese
Only when we were at home
Or privately with other Koreans
Could we fearfully break this law

The Korean girl couldn't relate
She could hardly understand the story
Korea seemed so distant
Her only Korean communication with her grandma
Her parents were too busy at work

She only spoke English with her friends
Even at church English was the language among her peers
Now she remembered
In the midst of thousands of Korean faces
The dead grandma emphasizing Korean culture

Learn Korean
It's a privilege
We couldn't do it

Because the Japanese wouldn't let us
You don't know how blessed you are

She took it for granted
Way back when
Her grandmother used to nag her so
She complained and complained
But now she missed her grandma

The love that she gave
The familiarity with which she was nosy
And all the gratuitous advice
On friendship and marriage
You have to marry Korean!

She sat there among the Korean people
In an area where not many Koreans live
An island in the vast sea
Like her neighborhood back home
A room filled with Korean faces

She felt a strange connection
A kind of comfort
Like she belonged
And she remembered the words of her grandma
How she said don't forget you are Korean

"Han River"

Han River overflowed
Throughout the city of Seoul
Soul of Han
People of Han
Drenched in overflowing waters

Heaven opened up
Dumping Han-ridden load
Waters carrying off many to the netherworld
Han of the people growing
Han everywhere

Orange
The warning reads
About to turn red
Who knew
The rains would kill so many?

Sky and its Han
Who has upset Heaven?
The waters flowed
Like River Han
From the sky to earth

Seoul lost its soul
Why else would it receive Heavenly Han
The displeasure of Nature
Where can they escape
From the heavenly Han?

A boy asks
Did we insult God?
Did we offend his representative?

Did we bring hunger to God's agent?
Refused to give him what is owed?

Adults were too busy
Worrying to pay attention
They turned on the news
Watched TV
And thought that would solve the problem

"Have No English"

Have no English
I heard the Korean grocer say
With a frown in his face

As the end of a loaded gun
Poked him in the face
Give us all your money

Have no English
The defiance of hard earned cash
Inside that lifeless cashbox

And shake it did
The loaded gun
Ready to let out the smoke

Have no English
Shaking of the head
Hands glued to the stomach

Bang
Did the gun go off
Taking the head of the Korean grocer

Have no English
I imagined him to say
As his wearied breath waned

H. C. Kim

"Her Hair"

How does she get her hair to stay there
Stationary even as she moves her body
Even when she runs her fingers through it
They are static

How much hairspray?
Maybe it's all those years of pressure
Of being an Asian in a white world
Trying to get to where she is

A professor with dignity
Trying to fight for her place
Which she has already won
But which she feels is still not her own

She controls one thing that she can
Her hair from moving
And reminding her of her fleeting place
She imagines is insecure in white academia

"Her Skin"

She looked at her skin and wondered
Why her skin was so yellowish
And not pure white like her friend's

She thought about what her friend said
That she is beautiful in her own way
What does that mean?

Day in and day out
She went to her school
Not thinking about the color of her skin

A superficial comment
Awakened her being
To the reality of her color

Her friend meant well
She's a nice Lutheran gal
Who doesn't have an evil bone in her body

But the comment struck
Deep under her skin
The Korean-American girl previously unaware

She woke to a reality
From her dream
That her color did not matter

In the world of dreams
Sure they don't
But this is the Real World

She looked at her skin

H. C. Kim

And intently looked at its color
It looked more and more yellow

"Holy Be Your Name"

Hallowed be thy name
The young boy uttered
As his 13 year old hands
Grabbed the rifle
To kill the enemy

He knew he may be caught
He knew they may shoot him dead
He knew he could go to jail
He may even be tortured
But he wasn't going to give up his duty

Jesus loves me
This I know
For the Bible tells me so
Little ones to Him belong
The boy sang smelling gun power

This little thing
I will do for you
For I promised to love you
With my heart and my all
Even to death will I love you

The boy grabbed his rifle
Fear gripping him inside
He knew that he had to carry on the mission
To defend the Christian church
As Communists invaded and attacked

Holy be your name
Like the LORD's prayer says
And use me as your instrument

LORD Jesus Christ
To protect Your honor and Your church

"Inopportune Time"

The boy remembered
At the Christian conference
One of the many held this summer
Among Koreans around the country
What his father had said

You are
Our hope
For you we work
We have come to America
We love you

He remembered
At the most inopportune time
As he transgressed
Beyond his wildest imagination
Conference fee paid for by his dad

An Elder at the church
Who wants him to be a doctor
To be a medical missionary
To North Korea
To save the Korean people

He remembered
When he did not want to remember
How much he was touched by his dad
Giving him the testimony of his whole life
Lived for his sake so he could do good

He had sworn
That he will get into Harvard
Become a doctor

Make his father happy
Glorify God

But here he was
Having forgotten
Gone so far away from it all
Going along
To get along

But he remembered
At the most inopportune time
What he had sworn to himself
To do for his dad
And for the glory of God

"Inside the Dry Cleaner's"

She sat in her room
Looking at her face
Having become worn
Through all the years
Inside the Dry Cleaner's

Tear drop rolling down her face
Marring her image in the mirror
Through tear-filled eyes
She gazed at herself
And remembered the beauty of her youth

The college years
When her husband
Wooed her with sweet words
Promising her the world
A life of complete happiness

Why don't we go to America?
She heard her husband say
It's the land of opportunities
For our children to be born to us
Let's go for their sake

Not knowing a word of English
She showed enthusiasm
For the sake of her unborn children
To give them the best education
The world could offer

Hour after hour
Not knowing English
Being teased for her accent

She toiled alongside her husband
For the sake of her children

Now growing up
Even forgetting Korean
And the love for them
Which kept her going
Through hours and hours of labor

She looked at herself in the mirror
How quickly the time passed by!
She thought looking at her wrinkled hands
Which had folded one too many shirts
For the sake of her children

Tears welled up
As she thought of what her children had become
Ungrateful for her sacrifice
Throwing away the Korean ways
And engaged to a white man

"Into Temptation"

Into temptation
The government officials led them
Like sheep without a shepherd
They were all led astray

Christ will forgive you
If he is really a loving God
One sin will not send you to hell
There is eternal security you say

The government officials bribed
Christian clergy to expound
A principle in support of the government
Although the government refused to uphold Christ's Law

We are a secular power
We don't concern ourselves with religion
That's your domain
The government officials talked like the Serpent

It made sense to them
Into temptation they were led
Like sheep without a shepherd
They went along to get along

The fact that our laws support
Things that are fundamentally opposed to the Bible
Should not trouble you
We are a government for all people

Not just Christians
Live in our domain
We have to protect all religions

We are about tolerance

Then, why do you spy on devout Christians
And persecute those who follow Christ exclusively?
Because that is intolerance
And we are a tolerant nation

It made sense to them
The Christian clergy
Who submitted to secular authority
Like sheep led to the slaughter house of God

We are at war
We are trying to protect all the citizens
You have to help us
Help you

Into temptation
The government officials led them
Christian leaders
Who were not centered on the Word of God

They did not know
What the Body of Christ was
Nor understood what it meant
For Christ to be King of kings

What?
The Kingdom of Christ?
Isn't that like heaven?
They talked in their total ignorance

Into temptation
The Christian clergy
Led their church members
How could they know better?

It's been a while
Since the Reformation
When each Christian
Tested their clergy

Who knew the Bible?
God is a tolerant God
God loves everyone
Obviously they don't know God who kills

Joshua
Judges
I Samuel
Jeremiah

But it all sounded good
God loves
The nation is tolerant
Church will submit to the government

Into temptation
The government officials led the clergy
Into temptation
The clergy led the church members

Into temptation
The nation was led
Into temptation
Everyone became guilty

No one was righteous
Not even one
As Korean churches placed
Japanese national symbol in their church

Japan was not a nation
That pushed Christian laws
Or protected the Christian church
As abomination entered Christian worship

Into temptation
Government officials led them
Even those calling themselves Christian
And the Korean Church became utterly corrupt

"Is the Kingdom"

Is the kingdom really ours?
Or should we let the government control it?
A gathering of Koreans
Questioned Japan's dominance in their own land

This is a country of Koreans
Most of us are Koreans
Except for the Japanese elite
Which thinks it has a claim on our land

Should the 2 per cent control the 98 per cent?
This is historically a Korean land
It was founded on Korean principles
It was meant to benefit Koreans

Why should we cowtow to Japanese power
Manipulated by their devious design
Bullying good people to do their heed
Threatening as they go on

Is the kingdom really ours?
Koreans living in our land
Like strangers who have no control
Future destiny in devious hands

Why should we remain silent
As the Japanese elite throws their money
To lobby Korean weaklings to do their bid
And disenfranchise us in our own land?

Let us rise
And stand together
To resist the elite power of Japan

Which seeks to destroy our heritage

"It Wasn't the Car"

It wasn't the car
I heard his son say
Voice of a boy

Shaking in disbelief
Or grief
He did not yet understand

It wasn't the car
He repeated motionlessly
Asserting his toughness

His motionless face
Pale like the lifeless body
That lies dead over there

It wasn't the car
He tried to convince himself
Wanting to be rational like adults

He looked down at his toes
Covered by the designer sneakers
His dad bought him the night before

It wasn't the car
Rang out sounds from his frame
Like the sound of the fourth bullet in his dad's head

He didn't know
Why his dad did not just give the car
To the carjacker who took his life instead

It wasn't the car

H. C. Kim

He didn't die for the car
Now the new man of the house tried to convince himself

"Japanese Informers"

There were Japanese informers everywhere
To incriminate Koreans
To produce dubious evidence against them
Japanese people hated Koreans

So the Koreans thought
Living under Japanese Occupation
Japanese police officers abusing their power
Japanese people informing the police at every turn

Koreans hated Japanese people
And wanted every Japanese people dead
Even the newborn baby in a Japanese woman's arm
Next to her a Japanese informer against Koreans

Koreans lived in fear
Because Japanese worked to put them there
Japan did not want to get along
They just wanted to spite the Koreans

There were Japanese informers in every corner
Ready to accuse Koreans
To find fault with Koreans
To lie about Korean people's character

Koreans hated the Japanese
And wanted every Japanese person dead
Including the little baby in her mother's arms
It was her husband who shot the Korean dead

So the Koreans plotted against the Japanese
Informers, police, all Japanese individuals
To kill them when they least expected

But atom bombs beat them to the punch

"Japanese Police"

The Japanese Police sounded their alarm
To entrap Koreans
Just to fault them
To put them down

They patrolled the street
With nothing better to do
Than harass Koreans
Who had become vulnerable

They thought they could intimidate
Put an easy trap for them
Get some Japanese to testify against them
Japan was united against Koreans

Colonialist power at its strength
There was no righteousness in the land
Japan added injustice upon injustice
Making a secret pact to do evil

Will not the Heavens judge them
And kill their innocent civilians
Like they harassed Korea's innocent
Making them lose sleep at night?

Koreans prayed for justice
For God to do to the Japanese
What Japan has done to Koreans
Vengeance is Mine saith the LORD

"Japanese Testimony"

Japanese testimonies were on record
Little did they know
That would bring about their destruction
They signed their names
And left a message of their identity

Stupidly they testified
Thinking that Japanese police could protect them
Didn't they know?
Japanese police were hated there
So were the Japanese mayors

It was only a matter of time
Before they drove the Japanese from the land
They left a record of their evil treacherous deeds
Names signed on testimonies meant to be against Koreans
Which will be used against them the testifiers eventually

How stupid could they be?
Signing their names on the dotted line
To testify against their own people in the land
Did they not know?
The Japanese are a people hated here in Korealand

"Koreatown"

Koreatown in downtown LA
Smack in the middle of business
LA culture
California wealth

Korean restaurants filled with Koreans
Korean shops filled with Hispanics
Korean squares filled with African-Americans
Korean places filled with color

Where are the whites of Los Angeles
Who seem visibly missing
From Korean places
In Los Angeles Koreatown

They are over there
In the white areas of LA
Where they speak the white language
And do white things

Koreatown in downtown LA
Is for people of color
And over there are places for white folk
Where not many color folk can be found

H. C. Kim

"Korean Outreach"

There is a wide spread Korean presence
In Los Angeles in Southern Cal
From Koreatown all the way
To Venice Beach
And down the coast

The center of Korean presence
In the United States
Is Los Angeles
Where over a million Koreans live
There are over 1,300 Korean churches here

Even when you visit Hollywood
Chinese Theatre with all the footprints
You'll see Korean shop owners nearby
Speaking in Korean
Listening to Korean

They say that you can get better Korean food
Here even than in the Korean peninsula
Who knows?
But this is sure
There are a lot of Koreans here

Korean outreach in LA is tremendous
You can go and speak no English
And survive and thrive
In this wide area of land
Where Koreans are proud of their heritage

You can go to Anaheim
There are Koreans there too
Their presence is visible

In shops, restaurants
And places of entertainment

This is LA
Koreans everywhere
Spread out
For all tourists to see
For residents to appreciate

H. C. Kim

"Korean Restaurant Owner"

In Koreatown
In the City of Angeles
There's a Korean restaurant owner
A very thoughtful person indeed
Who has a heart for her son

Who also works in her restaurant
When he can away from his studies
At the local university
In Southern California
He loves his mom

The mother loves her son
And wishes for the best
That she can offer
That her restaurant can proffer
America can give

He works hard
Understanding her love
All the sacrifice that she has given
On his behalf
He wants to succeed in the USA

His mother wants her son's success
For him and his future
Not for her own sake
But out of her motherly love for him
The womb that bore him

She questions how her son might succeed
In this new land that she has come to call her own
For you see, she doesn't know

How this country operates
This new culture rotates

She is thus left
With questions after questions
To ask how she might help him
The apple of her eye
How he might reach his potential

H. C. Kim

"Korean Ways"

Korean ways seem so out of touch
The Korean boy thought to himself
It's so backward
And so foreign to me

He thought himself to be American
Like his white friends in school
He prided himself in his perfect English
All the white friends he had

But one day
He went to his best friend's home
And there she hugged his mom
She called him her second son

He smiled and shared his plan
Of how he wanted to marry a blonde
And live happily ever after
With American dream fulfilled

He could never forget what she said
I love you, you know that
And because I love you, I will say
Marry your own kind – that's for best

The Korean boy's world was turned upside down
His American dream dashed
He faced the reality of his identity
He is visibly Korean, you see

He explored the Korean ways
Which seemed so foreign to him
For he realized no mater how assimilated

He will always look different

"Koreans Hear"

What do Koreans hear
When North Korea is condemned by non-Koreans?

Korea hatred a Korean bashing
They can't help it being who they are

Hundreds of thousands have their cousins
In North Korea, divided by the Cold War

For decades have Koreans in the South
Longed for access to North Korea to their family

Why do you suppose
Koreans use the term Korea?

Neither North nor South
They would like to put in front of Korea

Seoul, Korea
Many Koreans write in their letters

Seoul, Korea
Many academics describe their home

Seoul, Korea
Many Korean immigrants call their place of origin

Why?
They long for a united Korea

They can't afford psychologically
To divide Korea in two even in words

And you condemn North Korea?
What do you think Koreans hear?

You want to kill North Koreans
Family members, cousins?

It's one thing for the South to fight the North
It's another for outsiders to come in and mettle

Don't you know?
Koreans have solidarity, including those in the North

"Koreaspeak"

I hear Koreaspeak
Filling the company of Korean immigrants
Laughter coupled with memory
Quintessentially Korean

Yet American
In the land that they have come to adopt
As their own and that of their children's
Where they hope to find their American dream

Koreaspeak betrays
Their fears and uncertainties
Of dreams marred by experience
Children hurt by anti-Koreans

They speak of their children
Their difficulties facing an uncertain future
Of the goings-on in the Old Country
And how it might affect the New

They listen to the pain
Of others Koreaspeak
In language they think
Will shelter them from a hurtful outside world

They nod in silence
Between Koreaspeak
Understanding the unspoken pain
They are united in silent Koreaspeak

"LA Riots"

Where did they all come from?
This crowd and that group
Armed with bats
Sticks and stones

Out of nowhere
From the midst of darkness
They emerged
The strong set ready to destroy

Helpless in their own town
Korean merchants waited
The inevitable strike
An assault against their American dream

They had worked 15 hours per day
Bringing fresh fruits and vegetables
Goods and services
Which no other race wanted to

Korean merchants of Los Angeles
They treated their customers like human beings
And made sure they offered the best they could
When other races treated them like dirt

Yet, they did not understand
Silence was misunderstood
Korean immigrants can't speak good English
But they want to offer you the best they could

But the gangs kept coming
Blaming the Korean merchants
Who were confused

H. C. Kim

Why attack us when their beef is with whites?

One by one
Korean merchants stood in front of their store
On the roofs to protect their American dream
Years and years of hard labor

But the crowd kept coming
With sticks and stones
Ready to destroy and burn
LAPD do not protect Koreans, you see

Store after store was destroyed
In the Los Angeles Riots
Koreans after Koreans were ruined
Many retreated back to South Korea

And the Korean community is scarred
From the memory
The loss and the tragedy
The Koreatown is a different place now

"Laughing at Heaven"

They laughed at Heaven
In spite

What can the Heaven do?
They giggled among themselves

Day by day they went about
Mindlessly acting according to their whim

Korea is so advanced
We can create rain

People smiled rejoicing
Proud of all their human accomplishments

They laughed at Heaven
In pride

Week by week they ate lavishly
Carpe diem spirit has taken hold

Who can disrupt their lifestyle?
They thought it impossible

They were going to live forever
And enjoy every second of it

The New Rich of Korea flaunted their wealth
And thought themselves to be gods

They laughed at Heaven
In mock

H. C. Kim

We control the heavens and the skies
All the transport that pass above

We control the earth and its peoples
They do our bidding without protest

They thought they ruled over the rulers
And no one was there to stop them

But the rains came and came
The dead numbers started to add up

They no longer laughed at Heaven
As they could no longer see it through the rain

"Lead Us Not"

Lead us not
Into the ways of secular power
Abusing their government authority
To place their agents in the holy church
Jesus Christ's place desecrated by their activity

They are going to apply their secular laws
And impose their authority
Onto the Body of Christ
How dare they enter a worship place
And carry on activity on behalf of secular power

National government
State government
Local government
None of them has the right
To enter the church in the name of national security

But the Japanese colonizers did
As did the Communists in Russia
During the Cold War
Lead us not into temptation
To give into secular powers

In the name of national security
They insult the honor of Christ
Desecrate Christian worship
Impose themselves upon the Kingdom of Christ
Like they own the Body of Christ

Lead us not into temptation
To cave into government authorities
Who have no right to be in the church

To carry out their national security objectives
The church belongs to Christ

Lead us not into temptation
Lead not our clergy into temptation
That they will sell out the church
For 30 pieces of silver
Or out of fear like the fear of Peter at the temple court

The secular power
National
State
Local
Has no right over the church

May the government be utterly destroyed
If they stretch their arms into the church
In the name of national security
May you personally nuke them
This is the prayer of Christians under Japanese rule

"UCLA Korean Student"

The Korean smiled
As he walked the streets of UCLA
Looking at the Research Library
And Bunche Hall
Going toward LuValle Commons

He thought he arrived
Because he had a UCLA student ID
The goal for which he labored and toiled
Gave up movies and fun sports
Studied until wee hours of the morn

His walk was light
Jumpy, springy like an old mattress
His head was held up high
The Korean was a freshman
Ready to seize the day

Little does he know
What lies beyond those walls
And the struggles which he must overcome
Years and decades of Asian struggle
To gain empowerment that is far from complete

He doesn't know his history
Nor does he really care what was
He thinks that what he sees is what is real
Little does he imagine
There is true reality beyond the perception

"Little Girl"

I look at the little hands
Small fingers
That look like mine
My daughter whom I love
Who is so distant

Where is she?
Can she know?
She is so young
Does she even know reason?
Who am I?

The little girl looks at me
And recognizes her father
Or so I would like to think
And I wonder
If she knows the love of a father

Does she even know what love is?
I tell myself
I would kill for this daughter
But I can't quite get myself to admit
I probably would not

I wonder
If I have to choose
Between the life of this daughter of mine
And the life of another
A stranger or even a friend

I push my thoughts out of my mind
And just stare at the little fingers
Which look like mine, only smaller

I wonder if she knows
What a father means

"Loyalty"

Time has come
For you to decide
To whom will you give
Your utmost loyalty
To us or to our enemies

It's black and white
There is no grey
You stand with us
Or you stand against us
There is no middle ground

As Jesus Christ said
Those who are not for us
Are those who are against us
So, it's the time that you decide
Are you for us?

Time has come
For you to decide
Whether you will stand with us
And fight the enemy
Those who attack all that we hold dear

Our families and our faith
Our history and our traditions
Under attack by the enemies
Who serve another master
Who has another history opposing us

Time has come for you to make a stand
Will you stand against us?
And fight on their side?

There is no middle ground
You cannot straddle the fence anymore

"Martyr"

Martyrs
Korean Christianity is built on their blood
The young girl heard the preacher scream
What was his problem?
He seemed so unhappy

She looked at his face
And the blood vessels popping out
On both sides of his head
And wondered
Why is this guy so angry?

When the young preacher called
For someone to go to die in North Korea
She was sure he was crazy
Who would want to leave American comfort
And go to some third world commie country?

The boy stood
Good for him!
To go to the bathroom
Make that angry man angrier
Teach him a lesson by humiliating him!

Then she was shocked
To see her old man stand up
Walk across the room
In a room filled with over a thousand teenagers
This wasn't a conference for adults

See!
Even the angry preacher is shocked!
She felt a deep embarrassment

Followed by anger
He was going to abandon her, her brother, and her mother

She hated the idea of abandonment
She felt hatred
Anger against Christianity
Was it not enough that her father was battered for
Christianity here?
Now he's going to go somewhere to be killed for
Christianity?

She swore then and there
To do what she can to undermine Christianity
She made a secret pact with herself
As her father cried and testified
She was embarrassed beyond words

How could he do it?
Doesn't he love me?
Our family means nothing to him?
Like Jesus Christ, he's going to go to the poor
And abandon his family

"Meaning"

I search for meaning
To be Korean
What does it mean?

I left Korea
Long time ago
With my Korean friends behind

Surrounding myself
With foreign whiteness
A strange culture I didn't understand

Now, my mate is white
Spouse is white
I'm imposed by whiteness by choice

They call me banana
Koreans who see me
With my blonde girl and white friends

I speak Korean better than any of them
I would like to think
I am Korean

I would like to say
Inside my silent heart
As I smile to my white company

I wonder what happened
When did all go white?
Where is the Koreanness that I so treasured?

I know what happened

I forgot to check-in
Koreanness at the counter

"Meaningless"

Meaningless
Exclaimed the father
In the pavilion
Of his heart

As he looked upon
His daughter
With a University of California degree
Unemployed

Her 4.0 was worthless
You see
For the white employers
Who only saw her color

But he did not know this
For he was Korean
Educated in Korea
Idealistic about the white world

All this toil
I have worked for her
He said in his heart
Shaking his head

Looking at the daughter he loves
Who was contemplating
Becoming a hairdresser
Cutting hair for ten bucks

For the white world rejected her
Despite her education and achievement
For she wore a Korean face

A face of color unacceptable to the unjust white world

How was her father to know
Working 15 hours per day
To give her a bright future
Believing in the American dream

He blames her
The Korean daughter
For he presumes the white world fair
How mistaken he is

H. C. Kim

"No Korea"

As an immigrant I often wondered
What it would be to lose my motherland
South Korea which I left behind
In search of a better life in America

I know I am really tied to America
And with each passing day
The Old Country fades into the background
It remains only in my fond memories

Perhaps fond because it is a place of mental escape
When I face racism against Koreans in the New Land
Maybe I don't really miss Korea at all
I just need a place to escape to in my mind

What would it be like if South Korea did not exist
Either through military invasion or some natural disaster
What would I feel then?
Will I miss it?

As it is, it is only in my memory
I hardly visit Korea like most Koreans my age in the USA
When I do visit, it's a week at a time
Not much longer than that

It is as a tourist I visit
Not as someone who actually feel entitled
To the future destiny of the country
Of feel solidarity with the people in real terms

But I suppose I will wail and cry
Were there not to be South Korea
But I wouldn't really know why

Because I would still have my country

The country of my citizenship
The place where I was educated
Place where I work
And intend to live the rest of my life

H. C. Kim

"North Korea Missionary"

The preacher asked
Who will go for us?
To be a missionary
For Christ Jesus the LORD
In North Korea?

He looked over at the pews
Where teenagers sat
Startled by the preacher's sudden invite
Not knowing what to do
Trying to avoid his gaze

The preacher thought
He made an impact
He made them laugh
He made them cry
Surely they were moved!

The preacher asked again
Will you go for us?
To die for Christ
In the land of the communists
Where they need the Gospel?

Korean-American teenagers looked up
From their pews
As the preacher looked
Toward the other side of the room
Also quiet and unmoved

The look of desperation
Came over the preacher's face
Who thought he had failed

To move them
With the power of the Holy Spirit

As he stood in silence
Heavy silence hanging over the room
A small boy stood up
Everyone gazed at him
As the silence was broken

Will you go for us?
The preacher asked
To die for Christ
To save the Korean community
To bring the Gospel to the poor?

The boy looked at the preacher
Excited and nearly jumping with joy
With eyes wide with shock
I don't know, sir
I just got up to go to the bathroom

"Not Naïve"

The girl said in her heart
We are not naïve
You show us those videos
And we are to suck up to you
Like some sick sheep?

She was only thirteen
But she knew better
Than he expected
He had underestimated her
The confident Korean-American woman

Wise beyond her years
Product of her mother's guidance
Clever in a way surprising
A credit to her father
Not naïve as assumed

She was Korean-American
Proud to be a Christian
With a Christian heritage
That gave her strength
She knew the devil when she saw one

She wasn't fooled
Although she was only thirteen
She told herself
I am the future of Korea
I can stand up for Korean Christianity

Little did they know
That she wasn't alone
But there were many strong Koreans

The Korean Spirit: Poems

Proud of their history and culture
And most of all Korean Christianity

"On Earth As In Heaven"

On Earth as in Heaven
Death was all around
Sounds of guns firing
Soldiers in airplanes
Soldiers in tanks

The communists are coming!
People shouted in the streets
Frenzied by terror
Death and blood
Loss of family life

The army invaded
Like a swarm of locusts from the skies
And covered all of South Korea
Destruction and mayhem followed
Sound of death and pain

On Earth as in Heaven
Death machines rolled
And there was no quiet
No peace
Just sound of machinery

Who could escape
The all out war
Meant to bring death
And destruction
A kind of judgment

Are you angry LORD?
The pastor shouted
Why? Why?

And he felt guilt in his gut
A sense of remembering

You are doing this
Because we as clergy
Decided to let abomination into the church
Right?
Is that why?

The pastor heard no answer
You know there were many clergy
Who refused to bow down
They worshipped faithfully
And did not defile Your sanctuary

Many churches did not put a flag
Of a country that opposed your rule
Did not uphold your laws
In the holy worship place
Of one true God

How could you punish us
Like this
The pastor went on and on
Smell of blood fresh in his mind
His own wife dead by a stray bullet

We are mortals, LORD
We feared our country
And its agents who entered our church
In the name of National Security
We didn't disrespect you by giving them a place

The pastor talked to the empty room
The flag the shrine
They were to respect the power of the land

Don't you see?
The pastor reasoned against emptiness

He could hear death all around
As bombs dropped
The earth shook
Explosions everywhere
On earth as in heaven

Will you wipe out the righteous
With the wicked who did wrong?
Many clergy did not cowtow to the flag
But upheld the cross of the LORD Jesus Christ
Christ the King

Will You destroy our country
Kill our people
Because there are not 100 righteous?
That would be unfair
The pastor quivered as he heard no reply

Sounds of explosions did not stop
Bombs kept coming and the earth shook
Death everywhere all around
On earth as it is in heaven
Then a bomb struck the pastor dead on

"One Dead"

I shot one dead!
He exclaimed in excitement
My bullet killed the enemy!
He exulted as he looked at his gun
Still seeming to shake from the shooting

Those next to him looked at him
Some seemed offended by his excitement
Others turned away
He heard some people screaming
And one rushing towards him

I shot one dead!
He exclaimed
It was his first kill
With the gun that was brand new
He had shot dead an enemy soldier

Just 17
Drafted due to circumstances
This young South Korean
Had killed a North Korean soldier
Whose face he did not clearly see before the shot

He is dead!
He exclaimed
The North Korean dropped in the middle of the street
Never to rise again
In front of a building that he claimed as his

South Korea will never belong to him!
My country will never belong to them!
The 17 year old exclaimed

Still celebrating his first kill
His smile radiated through the turbulent times

"One Wish"

One wish
I heard her say
Is for the two Koreas to be united
Divided without choice
The two Koreas are victims

Is that true?
Is that your wish?
It's the wish of all Koreans
To be able to drive from
Pusan to Pyeongyang without roadblocks

Why should a people be divided?
Why should family live in isolation?
Relatives never seen
Cousins forgotten
Their children born without any notice

This can't be the desire of all Koreans?
You bet
Ask any Korean in Los Angeles
They want a unified Korea
Like the unified Germany we see today

Ten years after the unification
A North Korean can be the president
Of the unified Korea of North and South
Just like Merkel the East German
Who now rules in the united Germany

Koreans are one people
Who rather share bread
Rather than exchange bullets

They are family members
Same blood

They are not historic enemies
Like the Chinese and the Japanese
Jews and Arabs
Russians and Americans
Greeks and Trojans

North Koreans eat kimchee
North Koreans speak Korean
North Koreans look like South Koreans
There is a common heritage
Common blood

One wish
I heard her say
Is for the two Koreas to be united
Divided without choice
At the whims of western powers

"Our Daily Bread"

Our daily bread is our courage
Word of God which gives us strength
For Korean Christians have suffered
At the hand of the Japanese
Who persecuted out of their hatred for Christ

They picked on Korea
Because of the Christian faith
Which began to spread like wildfire
Hit by the lightning of Christ Jesus
Holy Spirit burning through and through

Christ gives us courage
For He loves us
To go to the battlefield
To kill the enemies of Christ
It is more courageous to kill than be killed

And in the Name of Jesus
We have the victory
To kill is a fearful thing
Who can do it
If it were not for the Spirit of God

Who gives the courage and the strength
Our daily bread
We need
To defend the church
Day to day

As North Koreans invade
To destroy the Christian church
And bring dark days to the worship of Christ

Desecration of the altar
Abomination to the pulpit

We must stand up
Seek the gift of Christ
The courage to kill
For it is braver to kill than be killed
And let the church burn at the hand of evildoers

"Our Father in Heaven"

Our Father in Heaven
Not your father
Our Father

The women in the church shouted
Tears dropping down
After burying their sons

Who died in battle
To defend the church of Jesus Christ
South Korean churches under attack

North Korean Communists rolled in
Mixed in with Chinese Communists
And they targeted Christians

Our Father in Heaven
Not their father
They do not believe in You

They do not belong to our family
The family of the LORD Jesus Christ
The women wailed in their prayer place

As more and more of their children
Younger and younger
Took rifles in hand to wage war

To fight the Communists
To protect the Christian church
To kill in the name of Jesus Christ

"Private War"

Thirteen year old boys
Started their private war
As clearly they conquered the country
No official resistance to be seen
The holy ground defiled

Our fathers are dead
Our mothers have been raped
It is up to us to fight
One thirteen year old boy said
He held the gun of a dead soldier in his hand

We need to defend the country
We have to learn to kill the enemy
As the Bible says
There is time for peace
There is time for war

There is time to hate
There is time to kill
The Bible teaches truth
The boy said
Tears welling up in his eyes

If there is none to defend our holy ground
To protect what is sacred in our land
Adults effectively killed
Others too scared to fight
Then, we will take guns in our hand

And fight off the enemy
Who have defiled our country
Invaded our territories

With no regard for borders that exist
We will shoot them dead

The 13 year old boy said
And another 13 year old boy added his voice
And yet another
And a small army of brave boys formed
To defend the country and what it represented

They started a private war
For South Korean government effectively ceased to exist
No one knew where the representatives were
They were hiding out in fear
North Koreans were at the southern tip

Millions already dead
South Korea almost all conquered
By them and their impious ways
Young boys knew what they had to do
To wage a private war and make a last stand

"Remember"

I can't remember
The smile
That kimchee used to bring
During the early years
Of my youth

When all I needed
Was a good Incheon kimchee
With some rice
And that was a meal
Fit for a king

Now I sit
With a fine steak
Exquisite appetizer
Fine desert
And foamy cappuccino to match

A company of white folk
Some who've never tried kimchee
Nor have even heard of Incheon
I am the first Korean they befriended
And I wonder

What it was like
The smile from that kimchee
One dish that assured me
I was a Korean among Koreans
With a pride intact

"Segregated Cafeteria"

I walked into the cafeteria
And saw it segregated
Koreans to the left
Whites to the right
Hispanics in the middle

I wanted to know why
And asked those in the Korean camp
They don't want us
The whites
They look down at us and don't understand us

I asked the whites
To give them a fair hearing
They isolate themselves
They want to be with their own kind
To eat their food

I walked to the Hispanics
And could not communicate with them
Because they were speaking in Spanish
And I thought I needed to know Spanish
Maybe I should have tried French

I don't know what to think
The conflict between Koreans and whites
And the Hispanic Switzerland in the middle
Who's to blame?
Who is right?

I looked at the cafeteria
Segregated by color
And wondered what the future will be

H. C. Kim

Of America whose melting-pot image
Has been traded in for potheads doing dope

And segregated cafeterias
That color the Southern California schools
Even universities
And perhaps places of work as well
What is to become of all this?

"Seoul"

I left my soul in Seoul
I used to tell my friends
And we would all laugh about it

Now with the passage of time
As I walk through the streets
Increasingly foreign

I wonder
If it is true
Did I leave my soul in Seoul?

Time seems to pass
Daily routine
Not disturbed often

Sun seems to rise and shine
A typical weather in Southern Cal
Although there's more humidity these days

Cars block traffic
Like they always do at rush hour
Although the hour seems longer than before

Now I walk the streets
To get my 30 minute daily exercise
And look around me

Empty streets
Cars passing by frequently
Shops looking empty

Where is my soul?

H. C. Kim

I ask myself
I wonder what Seoul's like right now

I walk to exercise
To relieve the increasing stress
Of being Korean in the USA

"Street Battle"

The street battle has started
As scary cat individuals finally found courage
Deep within themselves
To be heroes to defend the poor
The weak and the disadvantaged

One by one
They took a weapon in their hand
A gun, a knife, a grenade
They conquered their fears
As they saw injustice proliferate

Street battle ensued
Private citizens
Too pissed off to ignore the wrongs
They took matters into their own hands
Because there was a need

North Koreans have invaded
They held nothing to be sacred
They assaulted families
Destroyed friends
And cheated people of their property

They raped women
Mother, daughter, sister alike
And they showed no remorse
Normal people became indignant
That such people should be allowed free reign

Normal civilians
Found the courage within themselves
To be heroes needed in the society

H. C. Kim

They fought in the streets
And shot dead enemy soldiers

"The Bullet Wound"

He felt his stomach
And remembered
Bang!
He heard the shot
And then all went black

Struggling for life and death
All he could think about
Was the children
Who have forgotten Korean
And the respect owed to their Korean father

He had a nice job
A graduate of Seoul National University
A promising future
Living in a country of his birth
Where he understood the custom and the language

America
Gave him pain and suffering
15 hour work days
No vacation for years
And people who treated him less than human

He did it all for them
His children
Whose future he sought
He wanted the best for them
But his children did not understand

They forgot Korean
The ways of Korean
Did not know a thing about Korean history

Nor did they care to learn
They became whiter than the whites around them

He felt himself go numb
As he felt the bullet wound
Working in the grocery store
In a very dangerous neighborhood
All for the sake of his children

But they did not understand
They neither cared or tried
To learn Korean and their father's dream
A little work they shunned
And ran from the love that took the bullet

He felt blackness enter
And all went dark
As he thought of his sons
Who followed evils of America
And abandoned the purity of Korean culture

"The Date"

I see a white woman
Sitting in front of an Asian man
And I wonder what he's trying to prove
What she's trying to prove

There he sits with head bowed
Like a coolie worker in his shame
There she sits in her proper white posture
Looking without being rude at the coolie

She wonders when he will engage
Her in a conversation befitting her white world
He sits there with his head bowed
Obviously not knowing the white game

She blinks as he starts his conversation
Obviously disdain springing up from within her
Hidden only by the trained etiquette of her empty gaze
Trying to nod to deny him a picture into her feelings

He doesn't know
What to expect
Or what she is thinking
He's happy she's there

She has the upper hand
In this farce called a date
Where the Chinaman
Becomes contracted to be a coolie

And give her the currency
That she desires over him
And over his whole race

H. C. Kim

There he is giving into it all

He doesn't know how to engage
The white world with all the white complexities
So he sits there
Thinking she's really interested

He chooses this world
One mixed with deception
Lies and misunderstanding
And it's going to cost his race

"The Good Son"

The good son toils day after day
In his mother's restaurant
Korean restaurant in downtown LA
Wanting to do all he could to help

Whenever he can get away from his studies
At the local university in California
He does
And sacrifices a lot

Certainly in his mind
And he rejoices
In knowing he can give back
At least a little bit of what is his

But when he hits the books
He starts to wonder
What this New Land has for him
What actually belongs to him here?

He wants to succeed in the new home
This country they call Land of Dreams
To obtain his own
For the sake of his mother

Whom he saw toil
Day after day
Week after week
Year after year

Growing up he saw
How much his mother gave up
To work in this restaurant

To secure his future

"The Immigrant"

Full of dreams
He had before
Even as he walked
Through the slums
Fresh off the plane

For he envisioned
With his hope
Founded on myth
Story and fiction
Imagined

Little did he think
The aspirations
Filling his heart
Lung and mind
Would so quickly dissipate

As his hand calloused
Under the strain of daily chore
Never a part of the story
He heard or imagined
Before taking the plane seat

Here he is
The immigrant
Body aching from labor
Spirit dampened from fatigue
Yet he dreams

"The Invasion"

Like a swarm of locusts
They invaded the territory
That was not there's
Disrupting life and killing even more

Bombs fell
Here, there, everywhere
And body parts flew
Before children's eyes

They exulted
Our soldiers are deep in their territory
You can see our soldiers
In their green thicket

More bombs came
Targeting civilian sites
Houses and streets
Public buildings and public buses

How could they do this, mommy?
A little boy asked
Tears in his eyes
As he saw his dead father before him

They are bad people
Who have no respect for human life
They drop bombs
And initiate war like it were a game

Who are they mommy?
They are bad people
Who want dominate the world

Control-freaks who do not like peace

I thought they were Koreans
Like you and me
From the North
North Koreans

They are people like you and me
But their goal is to invade
Bomb civilian sites
Torture the lives of innocent people

H. C. Kim

"The Korean War"

Who can forget the Korean War?
Those who lived through it
Everyone lost a family member
Estimated 4.5 Million South Koreans killed
It was probably more than that

Rivers ran with civilian blood
Those who were shot to death
Hit by a flying debris
A target of a massive bomb attack
Dead bodies lying everywhere

On a quiet summer day
The enemy invaded
Without warning
And they kept shelling civilian areas
Many civilians died instantaneously

Death toll rose
Civilians not knowing where to hide
Bridges and roads bombed
Explosions everywhere
Buildings crumbling everywhere

Where could a family of five go?
Where could they hide?
The enemy was relentless
And did not respect peace
They thought they had the right

They just invaded
Initiating military strikes
On a peaceful summer day

Breaking the calm of summer
And the happiness of those in the capital

It was a horrible invasion
Supported by advanced weapons
And a will to kill many civilians
To win by any means necessary
The horrors of the Korean War

"The Mirror"

Strange
How strange
The way they look at me

I can't fathom
What could be wrong
What's on my face

I walk around
And see strange stares
Pointed at me

What do they see
That I cannot
Those blue eyes condemn

I walk to the mirror
To see
What's amiss

And find out
That I look different
An Asian in a white world

"The Model Immigrant"

I have been a model immigrant all my life
Says a Korean shopkeeper on Western Avenue
But what has become of me and my family?
My son and my daughter have no future

Because of the white world that condemned them
For their color
And for their Christian belief
They were leaders of Christian groups you see

But the white corporate world
Wants none of Christianity and the Christian faith
They were hurt because they were Christians
In this land they call America

Their exclusive claim that Jesus is God
Made them targets of white hatred
That wanted to force them to recognize other gods
Other than the God of Christianity

Should my son and daughter be persecuted
For their Christian faith
In this land they call
The Land of the Free

But the unspoken contract was taken out
Against them by the corporate white world
That wants no exclusive Christian God
The strictures of the Christian faith

They were excluded for their Christian faith
They were persecuted further
Because they were people of color

H. C. Kim

What an unholy alliance of attacks

"The Stranger"

He looked at his wife
Did I really marry her?
He asked himself

Then he remembered why
Then he relaxed
And forced a smile

In his sleep
He dreamt a dream
Of a life he wanted as a youth

He woke up
Sweat drenching down
His hands cold

He looked at his wife
Did I really marry her?
He asked himself, again

Then he remembered why
Then he tried to relax
But could not smile

In a troubled sleep
That overtook him again
He had no dream

Time sped by
And he woke yet again
Next to his wife

He looked at his wife

H. C. Kim

I married her, didn't I?
He tried to understand

Then he remembered why
But could not believe why
He blamed it on fatigue

"The Unrighteous"

The unrighteous have invaded
With their tanks
Airplanes
Sophisticated weapons

Who are we to stop them?
We are civilians
Who just want to make a living
And carry on with our business

They want to act with aggression
Out of spite for us
To instigate us
To violence which they love

They bombed our civilian areas
Homes of decent folk
Roads which take us to our work
To our relatives and our friends

They are the unrighteous
Who have no conscience
Or decency
Humanity

They invade like it's a game
Life isn't a game
But they don't care
They have already killed many civilians

They are not going to stop
They will continue
As their blood-thirst grows

H. C. Kim

Thinking they can kill with no end

They are looking to their powerful ally
To help them in their invasion
To help them kill more civilians
Than they could kill alone

They are the unrighteous
And their powerful ally
Will they be unrighteous?
Or will they act with righteousness?

Civilians are dying here
At this rate, millions will die
Civilian people
Who just want peace

Why do they invade?
And act with aggression
Making a concerted effort to incite?
Violence is their game!

They are the unrighteous
Who will take steps to incite
Violence is their nature
And they put the peaceful in the corner

It's only a few days after the war started
Begun by their disrespectful invasion
Bombing deep into civilian areas
Of our nation's capital

"The Voice of the Silent"

Have you asked about the voice of the silent?
Do you think that the North Korean population
Supports Kim Jung-Il?
Or are they just fighting a war
That they have to?

Like the Koreans who fought in World War 2
For Japan because they had no choice
Korea was under the colonialism of Japan
Instituted by backroom deasl with Teddy
Forced to fight for their colonizers

Millions of Koreans fought on behalf of Japan
As Japan raped Korea at will
Dehumanized their family members
Stole their property
And threatened their lives

They did not fight for Japan
Because they wanted to
But they did not want to die
They were human beings
Who wanted to live

So these Koreans fought for Japan
The ones who murdered their parents
Who marched on March 1st
They had no choice
They were oppressed

So the North Koreans march
To fight for Kim Jung-Il
Because they have no choice

North Korea was divided
At the wish of the USA

They had no choice
They wanted to be united
One Korea for one Korean people
They have no choice but to fight
On behalf of Kim Jung-Il

The voice of the silent
The Koreans who fought for Japan
In World War 2
Because of Korea
Divided by Roosevelt's desire

The voice of the silent
The Koreans who will fight
On behalf of North Korea
Divided because of Cold War
With America's approval

The voice of the silent cries out
Why?
Why did you deliver Korea to Japan?
Why did you divide Korea into two?
Why!

The voice of the silent
Who have no choice
Trying to survive
Make ends meet
And live

Their voice is silent
Not heard
Not counted

No one cares
The least of all the US Congress

The voice of the silent
Who will die
From sanctions against Kim Jung-Il
What is North Korea
But a nation made up of starving people

Why?
Why make them starve to death?
Because a few missiles fired
Human life is worth nothing
To these threatening sanctions

H. C. Kim

"Three Korean Women"

Three Korean women sit together
With gravitas written on their faces
On the first day of classes
One with a thinking cap
Reminiscent of the French artists
Slash philosopher slash literary critic
The other in a straight
Trade-mark Korean long hair
The other obviously a researcher brainiac
Whose hair belies touching water
For several days
They sit in silence
Absorbing the irregularities of life
Contemplating the meaning of their existence
Wondering about why things are the way they are
Searching for meaning
In the midst of hopelessness
That is facing their communal existence
And individual possibilities

"Thy Kingdom Come"

The freedom fighters took up a gun
Deacons, Elders, and even Clergy
To fight for the Kingdom of God
Attacked in the Name of Communism

There is a time for peace
There is a time for war
There is a time for friendship
There is a time to kill

The preacher expounded the Bible
Thumping his fist into the podium
The ground shook
As his church members armed for battle

In the Name of Jesus
We shall have the victory
The preacher exclaimed
Amen, Amen, the congregation responded

The Communists are upon us
To destroy our right to worship Christ
In the way He wants to be worshiped
Thy Kingdom Come!

Amen, Amen
Deacons, Edlers, and the Clergy
Raised their assault rifles
Pistols and grenades

LORD protect us
As we fight for the right
To worship Christ

In the way He wants to be worshipped

We fight not for our country
But for Christ the King
In the Name of Christ the Savior
Who gave us eternal life, Amen

The Deacon prayed
And the ground shook
With Amen screamed aloud
Assault rifles banging against the ground

"Thy Will Be Done"

The little girl prayed
For her father
Who volunteered
To go to battle
To fight the Communists

He was 60 years old
She was his youngest child
Youngest of 12 children
He said he was ready to die
To defend the Christian church

He had seen what happened
Under the Japanese Occupation
When the churches of Jesus Christ
Were abused by the Japanese
In the Name of East Asia Co-Prosperity

He wasn't going to hide
Stand by
As the church is assaulted
Once more
New management – the Communists

The little girl did not understand
Why would her father go to die
Leave behind her and her mother
And all her brothers and sisters
He said he will probably die

She didn't understand at all
But she believed
As her father told her to repeat

H. C. Kim

They will be done
God's will

Whether he lives or dies
May God's will be done
And the father held the little girl
She remembered him praying for him
Thy will be done with my beloved daughter

"To Testify"

He stood up to testify
In front of his friends
A room full of Korean-Americans

It was a revival meeting
Of a national youth conference
For Korean Christians throughout the land

They came together
To find God
And themselves

He stood up because he felt compelled
To speak his mind
And his troubling heart

He told of how he went astray
From one step, two steps taken too many
In the wrong direction he knew he shouldn't go

Now, he was so far gone
He did not recognize himself
His parents related to him in tears and bitterness

He didn't like what he had become
A Korean-American without a direction
One who pained the only ones who truly loved him

He stood, talking and talking
Listing all his faults and problems
And tears started to drip down

No one turned away

They felt his pain
Many identified with his struggles

And rededicated himself to Christ
And the Korean-American community before him
Parents praying for him at home for a miracle

There he was moved
Poured out his heart
And found peace in his mind

"Trespass"

Forgive those who trespass against us
They uttered in their prayer
As tears rolled down their eyes
Trying to suppress their han

Forgive them who trespass our property
With no regard to personal property
Attached to the dignity of the person
And his existence on earth

Forgive them who trespass our family
Waltzing in like European colonizers
Like they own our family
And all the intimacy that belongs to our family

Forgive them who trespass our person
With no respect
They pry into our privacy
Even our innermost personal details

Forgive them who trespass our body
Beating it with their hands
Inflicting pain
Like the slave owners of the South

Forgive those who trespass against us
They uttered their prayer
Which they were taught to pray
In the Gospel of Matthew

"Truth"

I stand before
Truth
That is the silent space
Between me and the horizon
And I look out
Toward the vast skies
Across the unimpeded space
Above the waters
Rising in undulating tidal motion
And wonder
What is Truth?
A friend
Or a foe?
Truth
Who is he?
Or is it she?
I speak
Knowing no one can hear
In the wee hours of the morning
The day after the blaze
That ravaged millions of acres
Just a few neighborhoods away
Is Truth near me?
I ask myself
Imagining the emptiness
Across the small houses
Flattened by the fire
Sparked by a lightning
Which destroyed
Homes of Koreans and non-Koreans
Alike
Were this water not dropped from the sky
Those homes would still be there

And the lives
Truth
I face
And look into the emptiness
I know I have to get back
To the fire engine
To head toward the blaze
Yesterday's that has become
Greater today
To face an emptiness of another kind
Who knows
Maybe in the afterlife
I will know
The Truth

"Unexpected Attack"

It was unexpected
Who knew it was the beginning
Of millions of dead lives?

South Koreans went about their business
People waking up to go to church
But wham, bam, the attack came

Out of nowhere
No one even thought such an attack were possible
There was no preparation

Utter surprise
The attack from the North
That was to take millions of lives

Like a chemical weapon dropped on an unsuspecting city
South Koreans did not see it coming
It was invisible until the bombs were dropped

Like biological weapons hidden in people's food
North Korea came with stealth
That no one realized until it was too late

Who knew North Korea could kill millions?
They showcased their weapons
Which South Korea did not even know existed

They had acquired all those weapons
Secretly as South Koreans celebrated freedom
North Korea was planning an invasion

The Russian support looked harmless enough

A few guns here
Some missiles there

Russian made airplanes
What damage could they do?
South Korea relied on chance

The chance that destruction would never come
The chance that the North would not invade
The chance that they did not have all that secret fire power

The surprise attack came
And like the fruit from the tree of the knowledge
South Koreans awakened to their death

"Victory"

The victory is ours
The young man said
As he was led astray
By the police
Who were loyal to the other side

We need not fear
For the Lord is with us
To fight injustice
Aggression against the poor
Those who persecute the righteous

Policemen looked at each other
Some nodded
When their superiors did not see them
They were doing their job
But they sympathized

Korean police
Hired by Japanese authorities
Visibly loyal to Japanese power
But under the surface
Some were true to their heart and their first love

Moved by the personal sacrifice
Born out of duty rather than hatred
One by one
Police officers joined
The secret movement of resistance

They kept their job
But used their job to provide information
Intelligence

They had machines and networks at their disposal
To use to attack enemy individuals

They faked allegiance
To the corrupt Japanese power
Which dominated the Korean peninsula
But in their heart
Ran the true blood loyal to their true country

A country
That was dominated by foreign power
Who tried to force Koreans to worship their religion
To cowtow to their whims and demands
A spark of light was lit in the police department

The cry of victory
Of one individual
They put in prison
Called them mysteriously
To true loyalty to righteous allegiance

One by one
Police officers
Took a weapon at night
To kill an enemy
If an opportunity presented itself

H. C. Kim

"What's In It For Me?"

I ask myself
As a youth grown up in America
What is in it for me?
For Korea to exist

I don't know what South Korea has given me
I guess I can thank God it gave me my parents
I guess I can thank God it gave me kimchee
But I don't like kimchee that much

I prefer sushi
It's healthier
Tastier
And fresher

Kimchee is fermented cabbage
For God's sake
Kinda gross
When you think about it

Hmmm
What will I miss about South Korea?
I don't really know
I guess I can say childhood memories

But I don't really remember anything from Korea
I lived my whole life in America
My happy memories are all from here
I have experienced my joys and sorrows here

What's in it for me for South Korea to exist?
I guess there really isn't anything
What the heck

To be honest, I won't miss it at all

"Why Hate?"

The little girl asked
Why hate North Korea?
America, I mean
Americans hate North Korea

I am Korean
North Koreans are Koreans
They are my blood
My relatives

Americans hate North Korea
They hate all Koreans
They hate me
And everything about Korea

They want to starve them to death
Imposing sanctions against them
Hunger-stricken civilians
Millions died in last few years

Why do white Americans hate us?
Koreans in North Korea
Who share our blood
Our food and history

The little girl asked
And the teacher could not answer
For he had asked the same question
Since he was her age

"Widowed"

The widowed mother looked
At the pictures of her children
Now all grown
Without a father
Who was shot by a carjaker

How was he to know
A routine drive
A regular stop
Surprise
Then a bang

He died on the spot
Leaving his son and daughter behind
With their mother
Widowed
Hoping they will do good

Is he rolling in his grave?
Happy looking down from above
All the good that his children accomplished
To support the Korean community
Their mother and their integrity

He struggled on drugs
It's not easy being fatherless
She struggled in other ways
She needed the fatherly love
And now they are

Would their father be proud of them?
He had toiled for their future
So that they would turn out

To be proud Korean-Americans
A credit to his community

What would they say
Were they to talk to their dead father
Be proud of us
We have become more than what you have hoped for
We are a credit to the Korean-American community

The widowed mother looked
At the pictures of her children
Now all grown
Without a father
Who was shot by a carjaker

"Wonder"

The boy sat in his chair
Desperate in wonder
Why did his father stand up?
To go to North Korea as a missionary
Abandoning his family, his church, and his life

Wonder seized him
Coupled with fear
But pride crept up somewhere in this boy's heart
No one stood up
But his father was brave

He looked at his father
With tears coming down his cheeks
Earnest confession
His love for Christ
And his desire to live and die for him

And he wondered the nature of his dad's faith
He had gone to church because he was a PK
It was expected of him
He was born into it
His family's livelihood depended on it

The boy had never given thought
Before that day at the Christian youth camp
What it meant to be a Christian
He did it out of habit
To obey his parents who cared about him

Then the body was confronted
With his own relationship to Christ
And the essence of Korean Christianity built on martyrdom

H. C. Kim

He committed himself to Christ
Then and there and was born again

"Yacht"

It is my yacht
Paid for
Licensed
Christened by me
By an expensive bottle of Portuguese wine

The moment I saw
That yacht docked
With happy people
Pleasant people
I knew I wanted one

I would make a lot of money
Just to have a yacht
I told myself
A symbol of wealth
Of carefree spirit

I worked
And worked
Worked like a dog
I did
This yacht's the proof

Now wealthy
With a carefree yacht
I am missing something
That is the simple joy
Of knowing who I am

About the Poet

H. C. Kim is a poet who constantly writes. He has written many books of poetry, including *Transitions: Poems*. He has lived and written poems all over the world – Korea, Israel, India, England, Germany, and the United States of America. H. C. Kim has held the position the chairperson of Claremont Poetry Club in California, USA.

www.ingramcontent.com/pod-product-compliance
Lightning Source LLC
Chambersburg PA
CBHW031144160426
43193CB00008B/243